MOM and DAD Please Teach Me

MOM and DAD Please Teach Me

A Companion Study Guide

by

Joe Wesley

ARCHWAY
PUBLISHING

Archway Publishing books may be ordered through booksellers or by contacting:

Archway Publishing
1663 Liberty Drive
Bloomington, IN 47403
www.archwaypublishing.com
1 (888) 242-5904

ISBN: 978-1-4808-1960-3 (sc)
ISBN: 978-1-4808-1958-0 (hc)
ISBN: 978-1-4808-1959-7 (e)

Library of Congress Control Number: 2015952347

Print information available on the last page.

Archway Publishing rev. date: 11/13/2015

Contents

Preface

This companion study guide is primarily prepared for descendants of African slaves. It is not meant to demean anyone or cause anyone to feel angry or inferior to anybody else. It is meant to enlighten parents who want to help their children with English and mathematics concepts at an early age. It will also help dropouts who realize they made a mistake by not getting an education, and find their way back to school. It will also help students at historically black colleges and universities, the future leaders of descendants of African slaves.

I incorporated a small amount of my immediate family's history to let you know the struggles they have endured and to emphasize the importance of an education. An education is very important if we are to achieve the goals we envision for generations of Americans to come. I have incorporated some of the basic fundamentals of the English language and some mathematics with problems and step-by-step examples of how they are solved. It was written to inform you that the time has come for us to come together as a coherent family to manufacture the goods and services we consume and profit from.

We must create jobs for our children and support the needs of our communities. This will inspire our children to set higher standards for achievement and help make a better America for everybody. Though prepared for descendants of African slaves, every American—no matter his or her origin, status, or state of being—can benefit from the contents of this book. I encourage everyone to use it to help them achieve their goals in life.

I call for descendants of slaves and descendants of slave owners to come together and make America a better place for everyone. If America wants to be the leading innovator of technology and set the example for the rest of the world, we have no option but to educate all Americans—regardless of origin or economic status. This country was founded upon certain principles that are highlighted in the Constitution.

> We the People of the United States, in Order to form a more perfect Union, establish Justice, insure domestic Tranquility, provide for the common defense, promote the general Welfare, and secure the Blessings of Liberty to ourselves and our Posterity, do ordain and establish this Constitution for the United States of America.

The American Principle

Our government is based upon a democracy for the people and by the people; the economy is based upon capitalism. This book shares how descendants of African slaves can come together, build an economy for themselves, and help maintain democracy for the benefit of all Americans.

As a descendant of African slaves, I've tried to understand why we act the way we do and why we relate to one another as we do. Looking at the history of our ancestors, slavery has a lot to do with how we see ourselves and how we relate to one another. However, before we can address these questions, it is necessary to look at a brief synopsis of my family's history.

Where Grandpa Came From

My grandfather came to this country on a ship with his parents as a slave from Guinea, South Africa, when he was a child. After surviving the long journey to the Carolinas, they were sold and transported to Mississippi. Grandpa grew up in the New World without knowing what would happen to him. Life was very harsh and stressful, but the family endured in spite of the conditions. They slowly learned how to speak English and cope with the ways of the New World. Their slave masters introduced them to God's Word and spiritual songs as a way to reduce hostility between themselves and the slaves.

The slaves learned how to compose spiritual songs with messages about escaping in the lyrics. The slaves in the immediate community understood and used drums to communicate with slaves outside the community. They planned to escape without the slave masters knowing what was going on.

You must learn about our history—from the colonial period before the slave trade to the day slaves confronted their slave masters in a struggle to become free.

Grandpa Shares His Wisdom

Grandpa used to tell me lots of things. He explained how a black man sold his birthrights for a bottle of whiskey. Every man will live under his own vine and fig tree. An empty wagon sounds loud, but a still tongue makes a wise head. A ship without a rudder will go wherever the waves take it. A rolling stone gathers no moss. A ship at port will never go anywhere.

He said, "Son, the road you travel in life should never be discouraged by looking at how far you are from your destination. Just keep faith in God—and continue to put one foot before the other. One day, you'll look up and realize you are only one step away. Never let anyone attempt to define who you are, because God created us. He has already defined who we are. Just stay focused on your objective in life. Reach for the stars; if you only grasp the moon, that's not a small achievement."

He told me to go to college if I ever had the chance to do so. He told me many things, but I held these closest to my heart. My grandfather learned to barbecue all kinds of meats, and large organizations would use him to barbecue for their activities. He made his own charcoal from hickory and oak before it became a commercial commodity. He started preparing and barbequing a week before the event began because of the large number of attendees. He bragged to his grandchildren about how the first piece of barbeque would not get cold before the last guest was served.

My Early Years

I was born at the beginning of the Great Depression (December 20, 1930), and my sister was born on the same date two years later. My dad died when I was two years old, but my maternal grandfather lived until I was twelve. My mother's six children were all born about two years apart, and the authorities wanted her to give some of us away or put us in a foster home after Dad died. When Mom said no, we were so happy because we did not want to be separated from one another. All of us knew what a burden it was for Mom to raise us by herself, and we worked very hard to help her. I was the babysitter for my sister before I was four years old. My mother was a domestic worker, and she said I will rake the leaves and burn them when I returned home.

Raking the Leaves and Burning Them for Mom

After the older children went to school and Mom went to work, I decided to rake the leaves and burn them for her. When she returned home, she'd be so happy. While my baby sister slept, I found the matches, raked the leaves, and set them on fire. I did not do a good job of raking the leaves, and the fire got out of control. I untied the calf that was hitched to the house, awoke my baby sister, and took her by the hand.

We went to our nearest relatives' house, which was about a quarter of a mile away. We had to cross a creek with quicksand in it, but I knew how to go around it. I don't know how long it took us to get to our relatives' house.

When we arrived, they asked, "Why are you here?"

I told them the cows were in the field. They looked in the direction of the house and saw black smoke billowing above the trees. They ran to put the fire out, but it was too late. Everything burned to the ground except the barn and the chimney. When my brothers and sisters came home from school and saw the house was burned down, they came to our relatives' house too.

When Mom came home from work, she saw the chimney silhouetted against the dark sky. She was only concerned about her two children who were left at home. She was so relieved that her children were all alive! But I had a fever of 108 degrees from this ordeal.

Mom got down on all four, kissed me, and said, "I'm not going to whip my baby."

That was all I needed to hear. What a relief! I suffered from fever many years after that. I remember waking up from the cool weather, standing on the porch at night, and not knowing how I got there.

Accepting the Burden to Buy Mom a House when I Grew Up

At the age of four, I accepted the burden and the responsibility of buying mother another house when I grew up without telling her why. It was the most traumatic experience in my life. Until I was twelve, I could not stand for anyone to talk about it in my presence without crying. I consciously observed everything around me from that day forward. I learned everything I could because the most important thing in my life was to find a way to buy my mother another house when I grew up.

People may think tragedies like these are harmful to children, but I disagree. This tragic experience gave me consciousness and awareness of everything I came in contact with. The way I responded to my associates and how the other children related to one another leads me to believe this was the greatest thing that ever happened to me.

Wilma Rudolph struggled with her leg at an early age, but she got over it and was the fastest female runner in the world during the United States Olympics in 1960. Helen Keller overcame a childhood illness that left her blind and deaf. She made many contributions to society. All things work together for those who love God; they are called according to His purpose (Romans 8:28).

I was more conscious of what was happening in my environment because of the tragedy. I learned everything I could from advertisements in old newspapers and magazines. I ordered books on how to break and train horses and how to become a lone Boy Scout. I saved my pennies, purchased books about Boy Scouting, and became a Tenderfoot. Because of the tragedy, I set goals to be the best I could be in everything I tried to do. If I could not give it my best, I did not attempt to do it at all.

Opening the Gate for Truck Drivers

We moved to another house after burning my mother's house down, and, I observed truck drivers hauling logs from the forest. There was a gate the drivers had to go through. Each driver had to get out of the truck, open the gate, get back in the truck, drive through the gate, get out of the truck again, close the gate, and get back in the truck before moving on. Since I could see the trucks before they arrived at the gate, I ran and opened it for them. To my surprise, each driver gave me a penny going and coming.

At the end of the day, I had about eighty pennies. I gave them to my mother, and she was very happy. At the time, a penny was very valuable; it was divided into ten mills. You could buy sugar or coffee for five or ten pennies.

The truck drivers realized I was making almost as much money as they were per day. They told me the first drive would give me fifty cents, and I was to open the gate for all of them each day. I wasn't looking for any money; I was just trying to help them. My older brothers taught me arithmetic at my request and how to look up definitions in the dictionary before I started elementary school.

Mom Taught Me about God's Love

Mom taught me about God's creation of humankind and the Gospel of Jesus Christ while the other children were in elementary school. When Mom came to a word she did not understand, we looked up the meaning in the dictionary. She told me about God's love and how He gave his only Son to die for us so we could have everlasting life (John 3:16).

She said we should love one another as Jesus loves us, and she told me about Paul and Silas being put in prison (Acts 16:16–40). Based on the testimonies Mom gave me, I accepted Jesus Christ as my Lord and Savior at the age of five years old. Based on my own experience with God, I know he is real. By the Grace of God, I'm still holding on to the faith in Jesus Christ.

My Early Childhood Development

Growing up, I kept an open mind. I tried to learn how to achieve objectives and focused on the things that were dearest to my heart, such as buying my mother a house when I grew up. I had no negative opinions about other children—or anyone else. I thought all children were focused on their objectives in life and striving to achieve them, but I was wrong.

Some of my peers teased me and talked negatively about me. I knew children like that were underachievers. For the most part, they lacked the verbal skills to express themselves very well. I felt sorry for the bullies. When they teased me or told jokes about me, I laughed louder than they did. They shut their mouths and were embarrassed. They told me I was crazy, but it did not matter to me because I knew who was crazy—and they knew I knew.

Someone visited our house and took a picture of my family and me. When I saw my image on a piece of paper for the first time, I wanted to learn how to do that. In elementary school, photography became my hobby. This childhood experience became a lifelong profession that allowed me to travel around the world as a photojournalist. I provided news, sports, documentaries, and human interest stories for the news media.

I saved my pennies until I had enough money to buy a Kodak Brownie camera. Someone told me that vinegar was one of the solutions for processing film. I put my first exposed roll of film in a jar of vinegar, and the film turned black. After that, I took my film to the drug store to have it processed.

There were no schools that taught photography in my area, or any other place to my knowledge but I committed to learning how to take pictures. I wanted to write a book about it so others would not have the same difficulty with understanding how to process film and pictures.

Booker T. Washington was an inspiring person for me to read about when I was growing up. I wanted to be like him when I grew up, and I asked mother could I go to Booker T. Washington High School in Memphis, Tennessee after finishing elementary school. She said yes. I could understand numbers in any form: fractions, compound fractions, percentages, division, addition, subtraction, and multiplication. Without being taught algebra in elementary school, I did not understand how literal and natural numbers are used together to solve mathematical problems.

I did not understand how to solve algebraic equations, and I was too ashamed to ask what I should do first to solve the equations. I dropped out of high school, which is one of the reasons why I want to introduce you to basic arithmetic, including algebra. If you want to excel in any branch of science or engineering, you must excel in mathematics.

Quantitative and qualitative analyses are necessary if you are to succeed in any important profession. I encourage you to take an introductory course in all branches of mathematics if you want to achieve your goals in life. I enthusiastically knocked cornstalks by moonlight and attended class by day to help my mother while I was in elementary school. We planted a garden of vegetables and raised chickens and pigs to provide the necessities until I became an adult.

The first ten years of my adult life were devoted to giving my mother money to replace the house I had burned down. I was thirty-one years old before I got married.

Growing Up in Mississippi

There were no televisions—or even radios—in most homes when I was growing up. I didn't see them until after 1939. I remember the first fight between Joe Louis and Max Schmeling in 1936, and Joe Louis lost the fight. In 1938, Joe won the heavyweight championship from Jim Braddock. Max Schmeling was confident that he could take the heavyweight crown back to Germany because he had beaten Joe Louis in the first fight, and they arranged to fight again.

My uncle and his family drove their car from Woodville, Mississippi, to our house in rural Natchez, Mississippi, so we could listen to the fight as it happened. The whole community came over to hear the fight. They opened the doors of the car, and we sat on the ground around it to listen to the fight. Joe knocked out Max Schmeling in the first round. It was a historic and memorable fight.

Hitler was bragging about how his Aryan race was superior to all other races. Schmeling had won a fight with Joe Louis before he became the heavyweight champion of the world. Schmeling was sure he was going to carry the heavyweight championship back to Germany. The United States was pleased that Joe won.

When I grew up, there were dolls for girls and cap pistols for boys, but most parents could not afford to buy them. In order to make a wagon to play with, we had to go into the woods and find a small tree that was round enough at the bottom to make wheels for the wagon. When we found a suitable tree, we cut four slabs off the tree and put holes through each to make the wheels. We had to find iron rods and heat them in a fire. We bored holes through each slab by twisting the rod back and forth because we did not have drills. When we found a tree limb that was straight enough to make axles, we cut two pieces and put wheels on them. To stabilize the rear axle, we nailed the seat to the chassis and axle. We connected the front axle and the steering column with a large nail.

Not having things helped us understand how to make the things we needed. Need is the mother of invention. It would be nice if we did not have televisions, iPads, iPhones, and tablets to distract our children from thinking about how to make things they want and need. The absence of these things would help them visualize ways to make the things that are important to us.

Turn the television off! Parents should teach their children about Jesus Christ, how to spell, how to write, how to look up words in the dictionary, and basic arithmetic, including the concepts of algebra before they start elementary school.

My Childhood Influences

The most influential people in my early childhood development were my mother, my grandfather, and my elementary school teacher (Mrs. Annie Bell Ransom of Natchez, Mississippi). No one could tell me anything unless it was in accordance with what those three people taught me.

I may have listened to what others had to say without responding or accepting it as true until I knew if it was true. I knew my mother and grandpa loved me dearly. Mrs. Ransom loved all her students as if we were her own children, and we loved her dearly for that. I treasure my memories of her to this day.

A Tribute to Mrs. Ransom

Mrs. Ransom taught eight grades in a one-room schoolhouse. After her passing, we formed an elementary school reunion to restore the school and preserve it in her honor. At one of those reunions, I wrote a tribute to Mrs. Ransom.

She instilled a sense of devotion to God and country by leading us in the Lord's Prayer and the Pledge of Allegiance as the first order of the day. She taught us the fundamentals of reading, writing, and arithmetic, and she gave us a sense of purpose by comparing our quest for wisdom, knowledge, and freedom to the children of Israel's untiring journey out of the wilderness of despair.

Mrs. Ransom was a good teacher and a loving, caring person. She loved to teach and brought honesty and integrity to the profession. She encouraged her students to do their best. She used the art of painting with words to impress upon our memories a clear picture of an understanding and an obligation.

Mrs. Ransom had some uncompromising rules. Boys and girls may sing and pray together, but boys and girls shall never play together. She never promoted anyone to a higher grade unless they had earned it. She lectured us on the fundamentals of home economics and hygiene.

She said, "It's okay to be raggedy, but just be clean." She lectured us about how to make a toothbrush. She gave us a sense of worth and a sense of self-esteem. She told us it was okay to dream and take calculated risks. It was okay to fail—as long as we gave our best. If we failed, she told us to get up and try again. "You shall never fail as long as you keep on trying."

When we had children of our own, we often wondered where teachers like Mrs. Ransom had gone. Mrs. Ransom gave us a vision of what our futures could be if we took the time to look at the reality of where we were. She encouraged us to imagine where we could be if we dared. If we had plans and followed them with passion, our futures could not be denied. Because of Mrs. Ransom's honesty, integrity, devotion to duty, and unselfish contributions to her profession and the community, I proposed a memorial in her honor. The Annie Bell Ransom Scholarship

Fund would keep Mrs. Ransom's memory alive within us. Her legacy would bind us together forever.

My Career and an Unceasing Desire to Get an Education

When I joined the United States Army, the first thing I wanted to know was where the education center was located. I attended school at night because algebra was something I needed to know. I needed to get my GED so I could go to college.

Grandpa did not get an education because slave owners refused to teach them how to read and write. He couldn't afford to send his children to college because of slavery. He encouraged me to go to college. I paid close attention to every word he said.

A black woman taught algebra at the education center. I was under the impression that women did not know anything about mathematics. I found out that was totally false. She knew algebra better than any instructor I ever had. I absorbed every word she had to say about the subject.

The army sent me to automobile mechanic school, and after an internship at the Army Transportation Center in Fort Eustis, Virginia, I went to South Korea in September 1953. I supported the Air Force as a SCAWAF (Special Category Army with Air Force). I maintained their vehicles and repaired vehicles damaged in the conflict. Two soldiers in my squad had completed college. Ferdig graduated from Ohio State with a degree in civil engineering, and Benedict graduated from the California Institute of Technology with a degree in electronics. We became friends, built prop planes, and flew them. I asked them to help me with algebra, and they were glad to because it would help them remain aware of the subject when they returned home.

After they showed me how to solve equations, I studied algebra every night. I took a correspondence course because there was no education center in South Korea for military personnel at the time. My lessons were sent to Tokyo, Japan for grading. This helped me get my GED and high school diploma.

The army had craft shops, and instructors taught many subjects, including photography. It was just what the doctor ordered. I learned how to process black and white film and print pictures, which improved my photographic skills. The army sent me to photography school at Fort Monmouth, New Jersey, and I was a photojournalist for the United States Army for more than sixteen years.

I learned that Massey Ferguson Junior College in Atlanta, Georgia and the New York Institute of Photography in New York City taught photography, but I could not go there at the time. I was interested in more than just taking pictures. I wanted to learn how to create beautiful art with my camera. I enrolled in a correspondence course with the New York Institute of Photography, which taught me the ins and outs of photography. They taught me about subject matter, subject expression, camera angles, lighting, backgrounds and foregrounds, vertical and horizontal composition, and how to tell a story with my camera. I graduated in March of 1962.

A Staff Photographer in Europe

In 1964, the army assigned me as a staff photographer to *The Stars and Stripes* in Darmstadt, West Germany. I covered news, sports, features, and human interest stories throughout Western Europe, North Africa, and the Middle East for more than six years.

While traveling in Cairo, Egypt little black children were running after me and begging me to take them to America so they could get an education. Children halfway around the world knew what country I came from—and knew the importance of an education—while our own children had the opportunity but couldn't see the value of it. They were looking in the wrong places and at the wrong things for the answer.

During my tenure at *The Stars and Stripes*, I won several picture of the year awards. After leaving *The Stars and Stripes*, I was assigned to the Army Pictorial center in Long Island City, New York. I had the privilege to go back to South Korea fifteen years later to assist in making a film. The documentary showed the progress South Korea had made in the fifteen years since the conflict. So many transformations had taken place in those fifteen years, and many transformations were yet to come. We documented progress in research centers, universities, manufacturing, technology, shipbuilding, home building, and transportation. So many changes had taken place since 1953.

A Picture Editor in Louisville

I retired from the United States Army in 1972 and joined *The Courier-Journal* and *The Louisville Times* in Kentucky. I started as a staff photographer and became a picture editor for the *Courier-Journal* shortly thereafter. I attended night school at the University of Louisville, studying algebra and other subjects. Near the end of the semester, my instructor told me that I knew algebra well enough to get an A, but she would give me a C if I did not attend the last two class sessions. I knew the subject, and that was all I needed.

I took algebra at a junior college and earned an A, but another university would not use that grade from the two-year college. Instead, they used the C from The University of Louisville, which lowered my GPA. I was competing for a scholarship, and it did not matter after that. I went out of my way not to let anybody know what I knew.

The easy way out may not be the best option, and in competing for scholarships, GPAs do matter. While taking a course in American History, I learned about the Trade Triangle between Jamaica, England, and Africa. The English would go to Jamaica to get sugarcane and take it back to England to make rum. They took the rum to Africa and traded it for slaves.

That's what Grandpa meant, I thought.

It hit me like a ton of bricks when I read about the Trade Triangle forty years later. I could not control my emotions! I had to excuse myself from class until I regained my composure. I literally cried. Everything Grandpa had told me about his family and our African ancestors flashed back into my memory. Under the guise of trading whiskey for slaves, they got our African elders drunk, forced them into ships, and sold them into slavery.

God did not put our ancestors in America to be slaves; however slaves they were. He put them there to give their children and grandchildren including this generation the opportunity to learn democracy and how to make it work for us. All Americans profit from it by building businesses and producing things we consume.

During my tenure as a picture editor with the *Courier-Journal,* our photographic department won a Pulitzer Prize in photojournalism. I resigned in 1978 to become a full-time college student.

A Forty-Eight-Year-Old Freshman

I majored in business administration at Lawson State Community College in Birmingham, Alabama. The opportunity cost was great but not nearly as great as not getting an education. Athletes concentrate on being the best in their chosen sports activities, which is good, but if they fail to learn how to protect and invest their earnings from sports, what good is that effort?

At Lawson State, I volunteered to help my classmates with math and accounting when I realized they needed help. When the director found out what I was doing, she asked me to tutor all students in the college who needed help in math and accounting. She gave me a stipend to do it, and I agreed. I also taught a course in photography while attending college there. After graduating, I returned to Memphis and volunteered to tutor students at Booker T. Washington High School. I later accepted an appointment as a contract specialist at the Pentagon.

A Contract Specialist
at the Pentagon

During my tenure at the Pentagon as a contract specialist, I helped cut the cost of goods and services the government needed to fulfill its requirements. I wrote proposals that vendors could bid on if they had the resources to fulfill the requirement. I suggested that the government create an electronic website that vendors could access. If they could fill the government need, award the contract to the lowest bidder. This would eliminate having to go through the long process of writing proposals and waiting to get responses from vendors to see if they could fulfill the requirement. We invited them to discuss their responses before awarding contracts, and they adopted my suggestions. I tutored students at local schools after work while assigned there. I retired from that position in 1998 and moved to Birmingham, Alabama.

Volunteering and Helping Others

The World of Opportunity (WOO), an organization created to help young adults get their GEDs and help them get jobs, was in need of volunteers to tutor students in their program in Birmingham. I responded to the call.

Booker T. Washington Elementary School also at Birmingham needed tutorial assistance for its students. We initiated a tutorial program through our church, St. Paul Lutheran Church, to assist in that effort for a number of years. Knowing that some of our people did not have the knowledge or the correct information to find the path to a higher education inspired me to write this book.

Look at the path we've traveled through the centuries to get where we are today. Harriet Tubman led people to freedom on the Underground Railroad during the 1860s. The Civil War contributed to preserving this country as an undivided nation. The Emancipation Proclamation supposedly freed slaves via the Freedmen's Bureau. Later, the Black Codes enslaved black people for another hundred years. The government sanctioned the Tuskegee Experiment, which injected black men with syphilis without their knowledge, and when penicillin became available as a cure, failed to treat them. It is important to know our history and prevent similar things like this from happening again.

Descendants of African Slaves

Slavery was a way of life throughout history. Look at the enslavement of the Jews by the Egyptians (Exodus 1–14). Queen Elizabeth II knighted Drake and Gilbert into the Order of the Knights of the Roundtable for pirating gold from the Spanish ships on the high seas. My pastor said race was not the motive for enslaving people, and I agree with him.

Blacks were not the only slaves in America. White people were brought from Europe as slaves. Let us not focus only on black-white confrontations. Instead, let us seize the opportunity to demonstrate our ability to contribute to the welfare of all citizens in America. Don't rush to leave high school. Expose yourself to as many of the branches of science, mathematics, engineering, the humanities, and history as you can. The high schools that offer these courses will equip students for college, research labs, and beyond.

Be careful. Children who interact with other about their goals and aspirations may be led by some of their associates in directions they did not intend to go. When you depart from one another, you must travel the road that's prepared for you. Focus on the things you are going to college for. Use available academic resources to make this a joyful and successful journey. This advice may be the most important you'll receive in your life.

An Excerpt from My Pastor's Sermon

R everend Thomas R. Noon was my pastor at St. Paul Evangelical Lutheran Church in Birmingham. He happened to be white, but he struggled along with us in an effort to end segregation in Alabama for many years.

> The civil rights movement was not limited from the 1940s to the present. And it is not a simple matter of between black and white. Our country has a history of discrimination. Chinese people have been discriminated against, Jewish people, Irish,

Italians, Greeks, and Polish among others. Japanese Americans were rounded up during World War II and interned in camps. Germans in America were suspected in both World Wars of working for the Huns or Nazis. That's not even getting to the matter of treatment of the Native Americans and the phrase "the only good Indian is a dead one," broken treaties, slaughter of women and children, and placement on barren reservations. Blacks, on the other hand, were enslaved by their own or Europeans in Africa, bought, sold, carted, and boarded crowded ships for the long trip over the Atlantic. If they survived, they arrived in a new country and culture against their will. Declared less than fully human, they were subjected to be slaves to others and were deprived of the opportunity to learn basic skills. Most languished in poverty and were illiterate for decades until other Americans began to question this kind of deliberate discrimination. The author of the book of James is well aware of the discrimination problem in the New Testament Church. In Acts 6, Greek Christian widows complained about unequal treatment in the daily distribution in connection with the Hebrew widows. The problem was somewhat resolved when appointments were made to make sure this did not become a lingering issue and everyone was treated fairly. There are all kinds of manifestations, but the root cause always continues to be sin. The descendants of African ancestors should not look at slavery as a racial issue because it was not; this was the European way of life: survival of the fittest. The European countries adopted this concept as a means of survival, taking by force from those who had no defense against such tactics.

A New Era

The world is much different now than when I grew up. Our economy was based mostly on agriculture. Manufacturing was well under way in some areas, including farm equipment and automobiles. Electronics such as televisions, computers, and calculators were not in the manufacturing process for the most part until after World War II ended in 1945.

Most grown-ups made less than a dollar a day. They worked from dawn to dusk in the fields and in the homes of well-to-do plantation owners. The United States responded to the bombing of Pearl Harbor by Japan on December 7, 1941. This brought us into World War II, and everything from that day forward was concentrated on supporting the war effort to its conclusion. Women—black and white—went to work in the factories. They built war machinery, including planes, tanks, and ships. The men went off to war to fight until it was over and beyond.

Segregation was still rampant in this country, including the military. The Tuskegee Airmen had to fight segregation at home and in the military for the right to participate in the war effort against the Germans. The government did not integrate the military until 1948. Black people were segregated in the United States until 1964.

The Civil War

The Civil War was not fought because of slavery—as some want you to believe. It was fought because of secession. Some Southern states wanted to secede from the United States, and President Abraham Lincoln was concerned with preserving the Union as one undivided nation. In 1862, he told black slaves who were supporting the Southern states with their slave labor that all black people held in bondage on plantations would be free on January 1, 1863. The Emancipation Proclamation allowed them to leave the plantations and join the Union.

The Union had been at war with the South for several years without winning a battle. After the Emancipation Proclamation was signed, slaves left the plantations and joined the United States in battle. They helped win the war. The Reconstruction Act provided freedom for slaves for a short period of time. Two years after the war, the Reconstruction Act returned the South to military rule. This gave black people the right to govern themselves.

During the election of 1876, Samuel J. Tilden of New York won the electoral vote, but Rutherford B. Hayes of Ohio won the election by promising to remove the military from the South. He kept his promise, and Jim Crow laws reinstituted slavery in the United States for the next hundred years.

Descendants Petition
the Supreme Court

After a struggle, the descendants of African ancestors made a declaration that was heard around the world. "Free at last! Free at last! Thank God Almighty we're free at last!" Thurgood Marshall became the first black Supreme Court Justice in the United States, but before he became Supreme Court Justice he petitioned the Supreme Court, arguing that segregation was not in accordance with the Constitution. He wanted to integrate transportation, restaurants, housing, voting rights, and public schools, and he won. The political powers failed to concede to the decision of the Supreme Court until the Grace of God, the clergy, and other races marched with us and sang "We Shall Overcome," until the walls of segregation finally came tumbling down.

The children of African slaves have not fully understood our purpose for being here in America. This is another reason that inspired me to bring attention to the achievements the descendants of African slaves have made in America. We created the foundation for America's economic wellbeing. We fought in the Civil War and helped preserve the United States as one nation. We fought in World War II to help defeat the Germans and Japan. We petitioned the Supreme Court to end segregation in the United States. We ended segregation in America (to our own economic detriment). A future challenge is to create profitable businesses, educate our children, and preserve democracy as set forth in the Constitution. Can you imagine what we can achieve together now that the chains of slavery have been removed?

Let's Build a Good Economy
for All Americans

Now is the time to accept the responsibility for creating our own economy by manufacturing the goods and services we consume and selling the excess in the marketplace at home and abroad. This can be done by pooling some of our financial resources and committing those resources to creating businesses. We can make the things we consume and profit from them. A business consists of managing, financing, buying, transporting, storing, adding value, and selling goods and services to customers at a price they can afford (including a reasonable profit).

We need an understanding of ourselves. We need to know that God created us for a purpose. God loves us! If we cannot find ways to help those who are least among us, why did God create us? As an ethnic entity in this country, we must come together to provide the goods and services we need in our communities that are not being provided already by us. Don't focus on how much money we can make. Do we love the idea of making things we consume? This will create jobs for our children.

Do we have the sustainability to make it happen? What are we waiting for? Money could be turned over in our communities at least ten times before leaving it by networking (buying and selling to one another). This requires a holistic approach to our communities. We must look at how we govern ourselves—and how all parts of our communities can benefit by this effort.

We must plan, discuss, and ensure that all levels of our businesses will financially benefit, from the suppliers of raw materials, services, manufacturing, warehousing, and transportation. We can add value to raw materials and commodities and sell them to consumers to help them fulfill their needs at prices they can afford. There will be a built-in profit for all providers.

Some of us are looking for a train to buy goods and services from the descendants of African slaves. Others are looking for a train to invest money in before it leaves the station. All aboard! I can hear the locomotive as it leaves the loading dock. It says, "I think I can. I think I can." As it picks up speed, it says, "I know I can. I know I can. I know I can." Later, it has a different attitude and a different voice. It speeds around the mountain and says, "I can, I can. I can, I can. I can, I can!" The train is bound for the Promised Land! Glory! Alleluia!

"If my people, which are called by my name, shall humble themselves, and pray and seek my face, and turn from their wicked ways; then will I hear from heaven and will forgive their sin, and will heal their land" (Chronicles 7:14).

"My Lord said ask and it shall be given unto you, seek and you shall find, and knock and it shall be open unto you" (Luke 11:9).

There must be a reason for going into business besides making money. We must make a profit, but the foremost reason for going into business is to help those who are least among us to achieve their goals. There should be no stronger motive to going into business than that and making a profit in the process.

Sometimes we think of better ways of doing things. Think of the open-pit barbeque grill that left your barbeque dry. We looked at the fifty-five-gallon steel drum and decided to split the drum from top to bottom, put hinges on one side of the drum, put a handle on the other side to open it, built a stand for it, and put a gridiron inside the drum. This permitted us to barbecue with a lid on the grill that keeps the meat moist and juicy. We tried it and it worked. We did not realize that people would buy a portable barbeque grill with a lid to keep the meat moist, but we were wrong. After it worked, we should have made a design and applied for a patent. If we had ownership protection, we could have started manufacturing and selling them in the marketplace. We could have benefitted financially. We must realize that this is a capitalist society, and we must protect our intellectual property and financially profit from it.

A Business Plan Is Required

B usiness requires an efficient management leadership team with a good educational background in business management and honest moral principles. Entrepreneurs, investors and employees can make this happen by selling the idea to those among us who want to be a part of this enterprise. Several things need to be considered as part of the plan: Labor costs (personnel to run the business), costs of raw materials (materials needed to add value before selling), transportation (costs of moving goods and services to your place of business), storage (costs of storing goods and services before selling to customers), advertising (costs of marketing and selling goods and services to customers), overhead (general and administrative expenses), and training (costs of training personnel).

To defray some of the cost of training employees, the government passed the Job Training Partnership Act (JTPA). It will pay for some of the cost of training personnel—and sometimes all of it if you hire them after they have been trained. It can be on-the-job training, or it can be done at local colleges or universities. The Workforce Investment Act replaced the JTPA in 1998 during the Clinton Administration. Another act will probably replace it in the future.

You should look into government programs like these to see how they can help your business pay for employee training. There is a term in business called "unit price." The aforementioned costs (labor, transportation, storage, marketing, and overhead) are added to each unit based on volume. If you buy one unit—let's say a pound of butter—you pay the full price, which includes costs from each of the costs listed previously. If you buy five thousand pounds, ten thousand pounds, or more, the unit cost per pound will be much less because some of the aforementioned costs go away.

All major corporations have a "volume price list," which lowers the price per unit as the volume goes up. How do you think franchises can sell goods and services for less than mom-and-pop stores can? They buy in high volume to get the lower unit price, which cuts the cost for consumers. We can do this by considering all the aspects of our businesses and our resources and by allocating those resources to achieve the lowest cost for our customers.

The Field Slave, the House Slave, and the Slave Master

The slave masters initiated a division among the African slaves by treating slaves who worked in houses more favorably than those who worked in the fields. They demanded that the house slaves keep the slave master informed about the field slaves' intentions because the field slaves were planning to leave the plantation and go back to Africa. The house slaves agreed to keep the slave master informed about the field slaves' plans for escape.

Since that day, there has been a lack of trust among most descendants of African slaves. This is one of the reasons for how we relate to one another. We don't know our history. We don't know that slavery is the cause of our economic condition today. We must know our history and how we were denied the opportunity to get an education. We must know the truth about our history and reconcile ourselves with one another as we once were. We must make a reconciliation agreement in the form of a contract between all descendants of African slaves who are ready to move forward in planning our economic, political, and social futures. The plan must be signed to ensure that the bond is real and forever.

Signing a Reconciliation Agreement

Entrepreneurs and investors of descendants of African slaves who see that the time has come for us to come together as a coherent family must initiate this agreement. We will produce and manufacture the things we consume and sell the excess in the marketplace at home and abroad. We must invite others who see the need to sit down and participate in the planning of this enterprise agreement. It must be structured with the best interests of investors as a priority. Each share of the enterprise shall be given a dollar value, and buyers of these shares would be buying partnerships in the enterprise.

Children of the investors should not have to sign the

agreement because they are subject to the same standards of conduct as their parents through inheritances. The example we set for them to follow will be a way of life because birds of a feather flock together. This agreement will contain intellectual property, and details shall not be discussed here. An agreement is no more than a contract between two or more parties, and the laws of the United States sanction it.

This Train Is Ready for Boarding

This train is a symbol for a corporation established by descendants of African slaves. The train will be financed and owned by Americans who happen to be black. It is necessary to have economic, social, and political power to influence, create, and enforce the laws of this country for the benefit of all citizens. To do this, follow the instruction outlined in this study guide.

Descendants of African slaves in America must take initiative to build this train and let it be known that it is ready for boarding! This train will take the path that God has given us to reach the Promised Land. Get on the train because someone already said we would reach the Promised Land!

When we needed something in the past, we prayed to God for it. He provided us with the wisdom and knowledge to make it. Let us go into business and provide the goods and services for our communities. We can profit from it and make the United States a better place for generations to come. We are not Africans, we are not African-Americans, but we are descendants of African slaves, working and contribute to the needs of this country for the benefit of all Americans. Some of us would rather ignore the needs of others by trying to buy elections to benefit themselves and their political party. We should consider the needs of all Americans by advocating for inclusion rather than the exclusion of some to make this a more perfect America for all citizens.

Corporations Owned by Descendants of African Slaves

A business will provide the financial resources we need to educate our children. If the descendants of African slaves owned incorporated businesses that produced the goods and services we consumed, Cooper Green Hospital in downtown Birmingham, Alabama would not have closed its doors to inpatient care for moms, dads, and children. Instead, we would own the hospitals, and staff it with doctors and nurses of African descent.

We shall not be subjected to the same kind of experiment that took place at the University of Tuskegee. Instead of singing "We Shall Overcome," we will be saying, "Glory. Hallelujah!" We have overcome by the Grace of God through faith. We have the right to the pursuit of happiness as set forth in the Constitution by petitioning the US Supreme Court. We have the right to go into business, make profits, and provide financial support to keep services like these in place.

If the descendants of African slaves owned media outlets, meteorologist Rhonda Lee of KTBS in Shreveport, Louisiana, would not have been fired for standing up for her Constitutional rights. If the descendants of African slaves owned businesses, the outcome of the Trayvon Martin case in Florida would have been different. If we owned our own businesses, a Florida jury would not have given Marissa Alexandra a twenty-year prison sentence for firing one shot in self-defense. The jury deliberated for only twelve minutes (according to CNN). She did not try to harm anyone; she tried to deter her husband from causing her harm.

If we owned businesses and purchased the things we need from them, we would have the financial resources to build our own schools and staff them with our own competent teachers and board members. We would not have to be troubled by the harsh treatment Deborah Brown Community School in Tulsa, Oklahoma, gave to Triana Parker a seven-year-old girl of African descent because of her dreadlocks. This happened more than fifty years after the March on Washington in defense of justice for all Americans. Did the school board members of Deborah Brown Community School get it—or were they not listening?

For many years, we have tried to integrate ourselves into a country that stands for liberty and justice for all—only to find many who would rather see us denied the rights accorded all of us under the Constitution. However, we must forgive them. We know some of these attitudes remain as before, but are we sincere about going into business together? If so, let us make a business plan, incorporate it, and finance the business by selling partnerships to members of our communities.

We can provide clothing, food, housing, broadcasting stations, radios, televisions, and community centers. We can bring the truth about our ancestors and the struggles we've had to bring justice to our children. Power concedes nothing without a demand. Unless we stand together as we did during the March on Washington in 1963, we will be like a ship on the high seas without a rudder, going wherever the waves take it. This will create jobs for our children. This will create financial resources to improve conditions in our communities, create money for research and development, and improve the quality of life for all Americans.

Imagine the enthusiasm this will bring to our communities. Our communities will have the social, political, and economic power to balance the unjust practices that have plagued descendants of African slaves in this country for more than four hundred years. And when that day comes, we all can sing together in the spirit of the old Negro spirituals. "We have overcome, we have overcome today, deep in my heart, we all have overcome!"

Competitors and Employees

Be aware of your competitors. They are waiting in the wings to lure your employees and your customers away from you. Incentivize your employees to be loyal to the business by initiating a suggestion program for them to suggest ways to improve the quality of goods and services you offer and the methods in which they are served to your customers. And if adopted, recognize the employees by making an announcement and present them with cash awards.

Your customers will tell their friends about the goods and services they received and how they were presented at your place of business. Their friends will someday become your customers; there is no better advertisement than word of mouth. Create a spirit of enthusiasm and devotion to service among your employees so they would rather remain at work after the workday is over rather than return home. When your business has reached this level of competence, do not sit on your laurels.

Your competitors are searching for ways to take your employees and your customers away from you—without you ever knowing what is taking place. There were four people ahead of me when I tried to cash a check at a bank in Birmingham. The tellers were not responding efficiently to our needs, and I decided to leave after standing in line for so long. If unemployment is so high in America, how can this be? Why can't we be served in a reasonable period of time?

Banks are not the only businesses like this. I dropped off a prescription at a drug store and asked to pick it up within an hour, and they agreed. I came back more than two hours later, and it was not ready for pickup. This kind of action—or lack of action—is another reason to go into business and be a competitor. Provide efficient service to all customers and leave your competitors wondering what happened to them.

Where I came from, they told me the customer is the most important person in a business. Give customers what they want, when they want it, at a price they can afford—unless you want to go out of business. During segregation, black people had economic ownership of their own businesses. The black community supported insurance companies, newspapers, radio stations, restaurants, banks, hotels, and social gathering places because we did not have anywhere else to go.

After integration, we moved away from supporting black-owned businesses. Why? Because deep in our hearts, some of us were distrustful of one another from the days of the house slave-field slave attitude, and now there were other places to purchase the things we needed. However, it was to our own economic detriment because we did not have a vested interest in the black business enterprise.

We must make a change in our thinking and behavior

toward one another if we are to succeed as a coherent family of African descendants. My Lord said a house divided against itself shall not stand (Mark 3:25). So let us reconcile ourselves—one with another.

Descendants of African Slaves in Research and Technology

P rofits from these businesses could be used to educate our children in technology. We can build electric energy systems to powers our automobiles, trucks, buses, and high-speed electric railway systems across America. Educate them in science and engineering to maintain our lead in technology in the world. We would eliminate our dependence on oil from countries who want to do us harm.

There are more efficient ways to harness the power of solar energy, wind energy, and energy generated from the changes in our climate. Just imagine the many useful products we could discover: cures for Alzheimer's disease, diabetes, high blood pressure, the flu, and the common cold. We could develop collision-avoidance systems for the transportation industry, including a traffic-light detecting system for our streets and highways. Traffic lights with a built-in sensing device that could change the light from red to green when an oncoming vehicle approaches it going north or south if another vehicle is not approaching the light at the same time from an east or west direction at the same time. Look at the money we could be saving due to idling vehicles burning gas while waiting for traffic lights to change. We could use that system in Birmingham—and probably throughout this country.

Something comes to each of us in thoughts, words, or visions. We cannot turn it loose. This may be our calling, and we will know it because we can't walk away from it. It is not about making money. It is about losing sight of ourselves in the pursuit of making life's burdens easier so others can find their ways.

If you are sure this is your mission in life, take heed and prepare for it. God is love. Let us invite him into our hearts to guide us each step of the way. We know that all things work together for good to those who love God and those who are the called according to His purpose.

> For whom He foreknew, He also predestined to be conformed to the image of His Son, that He might be the firstborn among many brethren Moreover whom He predestined, these He also called; whom He called, these He also justified; and whom He justified, these He also glorified. (Romans 8:28–30)

> My dear friends, we must love each other. Love comes from God, and when we love each other, it shows that we have been given life. We are God's children and we know Him. (1 John 4:7)

Descendants of Slaves in Communities without Crime

L et us focus on those who are least among us. If we find them to be hungry, give them a fish. At the same time, we must teach them how to fish. When they are hungry, they can fish for themselves and be in a position to help others rather than looking for a handout. If they are thirsty for wisdom and knowledge, let us help educate them. If we invite them into the house of faith, they can become members of the brotherhood of love. Wisdom and knowledge are more precious than gold. They will be able to contribute to the community for the benefit of all.

We know it takes a community to raise a family, but we must not see ourselves as a community only. We must see ourselves as a coherent family. This will eliminate crime in our communities. Instead of focusing on ways to take from one another, focus your attention on ways to help one another achieve goals.

Close your eyes for a moment. Imagine growing up in a community where you could sleep on your porch at night without anyone attempting to do you harm. That's the way it was when I grew up. Can you think of a day when there will be no crime in our country? Look at the money we could save. We would have no need for a prison system. What would happen to our police? We would only need them to look in on our senior citizens to ensure that they were okay and attend to needs in our communities, such as teaching our youth about traffic safety, not texting or using the telephone while driving, and sponsoring and mentoring programs such as the Police Athletic League. It would ensure good relationships.

Will the day come when we can think of the police as our

friends rather than as our adversaries? This will be the day when all can sing together. "Glory! Hallelujah! Heaven has arrived on planet earth in the heart of the Black Belt and spread its wings across America! Now we can sing an old song together again. Mine eyes have seen the glory of the coming of the Lord; He has trampled out the vintage where the grapes of wrath were stored. His truth is marching on! Go tell it on the mountain over the hills and everywhere, go tell it on the mountain that Jesus Christ is alive!"

Moms-To-Be and Dads-To-Be

Moms to-be, you should not permit any man to have sexual intercourse with you without first making a commitment to marriage and a promise to teach your children to be the best they can be and by setting the example for them to follow. A life of an innocent child who did not ask to be born is too precious to not consider its future before conception.

Dads to-be, it takes a responsible and responsive male to be a dependable father to his children and his family. Any male can have sexual intercourse with a female and cause a child to be born into this world, but it takes a responsible man to know the need to plan for his family's future before intercourse.

Moms-to be and Dads-to-be sit down and decide what you want to achieve in life. What do you want your children to be when they become adults? If you want your children to be successful, you must plan for it; otherwise, it will never happen. First of all, we must have faith in a power higher than ourselves.

And that power is God through His Son Jesus Christ. Humble yourselves before God. Ask Him for guidance in teaching and nurturing your children. Set examples for them. In all thy ways, acknowledge Him, and he shall direct thy path (Proverbs 3:6).

You must have goals and visualize where you want your children to go in life. Prepare the way for them to achieve those goals. Where there is no vision, the people perish: But he that keeps the law, happy is he (Proverbs 29:18).

The Fetus

M om, the fetus must have a drug-free environment to grow and develop into a healthy child at birth. Whatever you consume, your fetus consumes. Do not drink strong drinks or consume harmful drugs before, during, or after pregnancy. In fact, it may be better if you did not drink strong drinks, smoke, or consume harmful drugs at all during your lifetime—unless your doctor prescribes them.

Eat foods that have the right nutritional balance of vitamins and minerals because the fetus needs them. Consult with your doctor about this before, during, and after pregnancy to ensure that you are consuming the right amount of nutrition for a healthy and well-balanced child at birth and beyond.

Have faith in God. Faith makes us sure of what we hope for and gives us proof of what we cannot see. It was their faith that made our ancestors pleasing to God. We may find ourselves in stressful situations when we fail to be in accordance with God's Word. Avoid them by keeping your sight on your objective in life through God's Word. Judge not the behavior of others that you may not be judged. Keep an open mind and ask God to lead you and guide you every step of the way to your objective in life.

A stressful person tends to eat a lot to relieve the pain that stress causes, but the only thing overeating does is make you obese, which is not good for your physical or mental health. My Lord said, Man shall not live by bread alone, but by every word that proceed from the mouth of God (Matthew 4:4).

"God said, 'Ask and it shall be given you; seek and you shall find knock and it shall be opened unto you'" (Matthew 7:7).

"And all things whatsoever you shall ask in prayer, believing; you shall receive" (Matthew 21:22). Since faith without works is dead, work for the things you ask for and believe. You shall not be denied. Mom, Dad, what are you waiting for? Get down on your knees and pray until the Holy Spirit descends upon you like a dove. Ask God for what you want because God is a Spirit and they who worship him must worship him in Spirit and in truth (John 4:24).

For as the body without the Spirit is dead, so faith without works is dead also (James 2:26). Work toward those things you ask God for. Act with confidence that you will receive them! First seek ye the kingdom of God (through His Word) and all his righteousness, and all other things shall be unto you as you believe. Learn how to listen, ask relevant questions, think, and communicate verbally and in writing. Learn mathematics and English as this study guide attempts to help you with. Learn how to dream and how to conceptualize those dreams into a reality by getting an education so you will be prepared to help someone along the way to the glory of God.

Items Not To Be Used or Consumed without Caution

There are many things we should be aware of and not consume or use because they are not good for us. Read the labels on all products. If they contain certain ingredients, do not use them unless prescribed by a doctor. Lead acetate is sometimes found in hair dye. Lead is not good for the performance of your brain and should never be consumed. They used to put lead in paint, but they outlawed the use of lead in paint in the 1970s. Be aware of homes built before that time. Interior and exterior paint should not have any lead.

We must be aware of the danger of mercury, which may be found in products today. Mercury is another item that must not be consumed. It is poisonous. Drugs that are not approved by your doctor should not be consumed. Anything that causes harm to your brain should not be consumed in the form of drinks or in any other form. Do not consume them without consulting your doctor first. There are more items that are harmful that I am not aware of; keep your eyes open for them and take heed.

Caring for Your Family and Community

Mom and Dad, you should want your grown children to be financially better off than you were. For that to happen, you must do something about it. You must dream about it and conceptualize a plan for your desired objective. Include education—and work the plan to its conclusion. Dad, your family needs a good man they can be proud of. Thank God for allowing them to be a part of your life. You must set an example for them to follow.

You and Mom must teach them academically and from your life experiences. Explain the good and the bad; explain how you handled situations they may benefit from. Align yourselves with families with children who have similar values and aspirations. As you teach your children, develop a lasting relationship with them so you can look out for each other. Care for your children as the need arises because it takes a community to successfully raise a well-disciplined family.

Your family needs a well-kept home to live in. Your home must be groomed inside and out. A little maintenance, such as primer and paint, will preserve your home for many years to come, and it will keep the community looking good. Community members want to stay together because they have similar values, including a well-kept community.

God Created Man in His Own Image and Likeness

And in His creation God said, Let us make man in our image, after our likeness and let them have dominion over the fish of the sea and over the fowl of the air and over the cattle, and over all the earth, and over every creeping thing that creep upon the earth. So God created man in his own image, in the image of God created he him; male and female created he them. And God blessed them, and God said unto them be fruitful and multiply and replenish the earth and subdue it; and have dominion over the fish of the sea and over the fowl of the air, and over every living thing that move upon the earth (Genesis 1:26–28).

God has defined who we are through His creation; why should we listen to anyone else who tries to define who we are? What does it matter what someone thinks about you when you know that you are God's beloved. From my observations, the only people who try to promote themselves as superior and more beautiful than any other race are the ones who try to look just like us.

I read somewhere that "black is beautiful," and I'll agree. And there are people who have confirmed this by getting a tan from the sun or from tanning salons. Do not let anyone distract your attention from achieving your objectives in life by trying to desecrate you. God loves all of us—no matter what rays of light our bodies absorb or reflect because all colors come from the light source. If you remove the light, you cannot distinguish what color anyone is. God created all of us in His own image and likeness; never let anyone attempt to define who we are.

Children Are Born

Parents, children are born with an innate curiosity to learn. Don't think they are not oriented toward learning from the day they are born. Infants are like sponges—absorbing everything they hear, feel, taste, touch, smell, or see—even before they can talk. They learn from parents' touches, tones, and conversations with them. Teach them. "For God so loved the world that he gave his only begotten son, that whoever believe in him shall not perish, but have everlasting life" (John 3:16).

Let your children know you love them by telling them that you are concerned about their welfare. Let them know you expect their behavior to be in accordance with what's best for both of you. If it is not comfortable, they will let you know by crying. If everything is okay, do not cry—and we will have no problem. These needs must be communicated to the children by talking to them as early as possible. This is something that must be repeated until the infants get it.

Infants are in a rapid state of growth, and they need to be fed with liquid food regularly. As a result, they need to be burped (removing air from the stomach) immediately after eating. Hold the baby's stomach against your chest with one hand while gently moving your fingers up and down the baby's back until it belches. The bowels of the baby move regularly and the baby must be cleaned, dried, and powdered with each diaper change.

A child needs to grow up to be an independent adult. There is no better time to start than now. A baby should not sleep in the same bed with its mother and father. You may ask your doctor about this, but we allowed our baby to sleep in the same bed through the bonding process. We moved the baby to in its own bed when we were sure the baby would not choke or strangle itself in its sleep. We moved it next door to its own room and bed. We kept the doors open so we could hear if the baby needed us.

Babies will sense that they are not in the same room with Mom and Dad and will express their disapproval by crying. Check and see that the baby is not sick, hungry, wet, or need to be burped. If not check and reinforce what you were previously informed about (what's best for both of you) earlier. I am giving you this advice after observing, learning from, and experiencing babies' behavior. Children will grow up and depend more on themselves than on anyone else.

Teach Your Children

Teach your children by singing the alphabet and counting numbers to them before they can talk. You will be creating a vocabulary in their memories. They will use this when they become more familiar in the use of language skills and as they grow and mature. Talk to them, read to them, and motivate them. Tell them they have the ability to achieve whatever goals they desire in life if they prepare themselves and are persistent in their efforts to achieve them.

Make sure their schoolteachers teach them devotion to God

and the Pledge of Allegiance to America, starting in the first grade. This should be the first order of each school day if constitutional democracy is to survive in America. Before we took the Pledge of Allegiance out of schools we did not have the kinds of problems we are having now. We now have school shootings and teachers carrying guns in the classroom. Is this the example we want our children to follow? I hope not.

Look at the example of the buffalo and the goose. The first buffalo leads the herd without knowing the destination. Wherever the lead buffalo goes, the herd follows—even off a cliff. In contrast to the buffalo, every goose in the flock knows the destination before they move. They communicate with one another and teach each other about their plans and the destination before departing. When they decide to go, they line up in an inverted V. And as the lead goose flops its wings, the geese on either side use the disturbed air to their advantage and pass it along with the movement of their wings to the geese that follow. The lead goose will fall back to the end of the line when it gets tired, and the next goose will take its place. They alternate and move to the rear when they get tired. This rotation continues throughout the journey.

Let us use the example of the geese to teach our children. When they get older, they will know what parts they must play to reach their destinations. Teach them how to think and how to dream. Focus on the things they want to achieve when they grow up, and as they believe, it shall be unto them.

Teach them from the day they are born and they will learn and know the meaning of what you have been teaching them when they are older. This is something you should tell them throughout their lives. Show them how to look up definitions in the dictionary and how to use a thesaurus before elementary school. After they start school, remain attentive to their academic needs. If there is any homework, make sure they complete it and turn it in to the teacher when it is due. They may get extra credit if they type it when they are old enough to do so.

Push them to the limits in a loving and kind way, and make it an enjoyable experience for them. The learning process can be fun and will help them fulfill their dreams. Do not try to make them into what you wanted to be. Help them become what they desire to be—and whatever God has chosen them to be. If you want your children to excel in art, that's okay. If they want to excel in another field of study, let them. Any art form must be loved by those who want to excel in it.

Teach them how to structure simple sentences, count, add, subtract, divide, and multiply before they begin elementary school. The first five years of a child's life are the most important and will remain with them for a lifetime. Expose them to much as you can during those first five years—without exhausting their desire to learn. It is okay to introduce them to basic algebra so they will be familiar with the subject in school. You will be surprised by how much confidence this kind of teaching gives children.

The Bible tells us to train up children in the way they should go, and when they are old, he will not depart from it (Proverbs 22:6). Teaching is a never-ending process. What you tell a child is part of the process of teaching, and the other part of that process is the example you set for them to follow. Children learn from observing what you do, and they aim to please their parents. What they see you do is a stamp of approval for them. Be careful what you do or say in your children's presence. It is necessary to turn off the television sometimes because it may give your children the impression that you approve of what is on when it may not be.

Early childhood training and development is very important to children's future, and it will influence their behavior. We should not let our elected representatives tell us how to discipline our children. Collectively, individuals are the government, and we elect members from our communities to represent us. We pay their salaries through taxation to make laws that are in the best interests of all of us, and we must hold them to that. Let your representatives know we use the rod to discipline our children only when necessary—to teach them what we know is best for them and their futures. Leave us alone unless there is child abuse in the process.

Children, Obey Your Parents

Children, your parents love you. If they did not, they would not go through the trouble of teaching you. Listen to them because what they are teaching you is for your own good. They are training and conditioning you to be successful in life. Listen to what they are teaching you. They have endured many hardships and have made many sacrifices to get you where you are. Take it upon yourselves to try to understand them. Thank God that your parents are taking the time to teach you because some parents do not. Some of your friends were not taught well by their parents, and they may feel inferior to their peers. The only way to get attention is to respond in a negative way toward their associates. They might not have the vocabulary to express themselves very well. They might feel left out of the popular crowd. When you see this kind of behavior, reach out and help them because it is the right thing to do. Help them express themselves by teaching them how to expand their vocabulary. You cannot make it through this world alone. We must help someone along the way, and my Lord said, Inasmuch as we have done it unto one of the least of those my brethren ye have done it unto me (Matthew 25:40).

After your parents have taught you the fundamentals of life and prepared you for college, it may be time to make it on your own. Go beyond what is required of you in your studies. Study everything you are deficient in and need to know to be successful. This will prepare you to face the future and succeed.

During your studies, try not to look at what others are doing. Stay focused on the path that will help you achieve your objectives in life. Form good study habits, study hard, and if you have homework to turn in, type it for your instructor. To help you recall information you have studied for an exam, write pertinent notes pertaining to each subject. And just before you lie down for the night, go over your notes. Consciously embedding them into your memory should be the last thing you do before going to bed.

When you are finished, look at your house shoes and think about what you studied; without giving a thought to anything else, go to sleep. You will be surprised by the first thing that comes to mind the next morning when you look down at your house shoes: everything you studied the night before. This was one of my methods of recalling what I learned when I was in college.

Two days before a test, go over all your handwritten notes. Just before you lie down and think about nothing else, look down at your house shoes and go to sleep. The day before a test, don't think about anything relating to the test. The morning of the test, do not eat anything until the test is over. I tend to do better on tests when I am hungry; after eating, I want to relax and go to sleep. When you are hungry, you are more inclined to look for something that will satisfy that craving. This will carry over to the test.

The process of learning is about how much information you can recall upon demand. When you cram for a test, the result is the same as cramming a file cabinet. If you cram too much into it, it will be difficult to get anything out of it. Keep an open mind. After each question, the answer will flow freely from your memory.

Don't focus on being the most popular person on campus or the big man on campus. Focus on the things you are going to college for. Be prepared to recall and apply those things when necessary. That is the time to absorb all the wisdom and knowledge that college offers. You will be ready to face whatever life brings your way.

The Alphabet Table

A a	B b	C c	D d	E e	F f
G g	H h	I i	J j	K k	L l
M m	N n	O o	P p	Q q	R r
S s	T t	U u	V v	W w	X x
Y y	Z z				

Point to each letter of the alphabet and pronounce it as the child looks on. Ask the child to pronounce each letter as you point to them until he or she can pronounce them all.

Make learning a fun thing by singing the alphabet song.

After the child becomes familiar with the alphabet, start spelling words by using letters from the alphabet table and pointing to a picture of the subject you spell. The child will learn how to use the alphabet to spell different subjects, what they look like, and how they are pronounced. Wow! Look at those little eyes perk up as they begin to understand how to use the alphabet to spell, understand, and pronounce different words.

Communication

Mom, Dad, teach them how to communicate by structuring simple sentences with them. A simple sentence is a complete thought with a subject and a verb. Begin with a capital letter and end with a question mark, exclamation mark, or a period. A single subject in a sentence must contain a single verb.

A plural subject in a sentence must contain a plural verb. We need to pay attention to our children as they begin to learn how to speak. Be sure the subjects and verbs are in agreement; if they are not, correct them by reciting the sentence correctly. As they get older and better at language, they will correct you if you say something without the subject and verb in agreement. Don't be surprised when they do this; just view this as an acknowledgement that they are listening to you and are learning how to communicate correctly.

Parts of Speech

There are eight parts of speech.

Part of Speech	Definition
Noun	A noun is a word used to name a person, place, thing, or quantity.
Pronoun	A pronoun is a word used in place of a noun or a group of words functioning as a noun.
Verb	A verb is a word that expresses an action, an occurrence, or a state of being
Adjective	An adjective is used to describe a noun or pronoun.
Adverb	An adverb is a word that modifies a verb, an adjective, or another adverb.
Preposition	A preposition is a word used to connect a noun or pronoun to another word in a sentence.
Conjunction	A conjunction is a word used to connect words, phrases, or clauses.
Interjection	An interjection is a word used to express strong emotion. It functions independently within a sentence.

Study the parts of speech and teach your children the same. These are the building blocks that help you and your children become effective and efficient communicators, writers, and speakers. A writer learns to speak effectively in part by writing. Writers can change words in their writing until they say precisely what they mean. This will help them become more eloquent speakers. Practice leads to perfection.

The Sentence

A sentence is a unit of words expressing a complete thought. There are four types of sentences: simple, complex, compound, and compound-complex. A simple sentence is a sentence with one subject and one verb. A compound sentence is two or more separate sentences or main clauses joined properly with punctuation. A complex sentence contains one sentence or main clause with one or more dependent clauses. A compound-complex sentence contains two or more sentences, main clauses with one or more dependent clauses.

Punctuation Marks

Punctuation Mark	Usage
Period (.)	A period is used to end sentences that are statements, indirect quotations, or mild commands and are used in abbreviations and within decimals.

Question Mark (?)	A question mark is used to end a sentence, clause, phrase, or a word that asks a question. Question marks are also used in parentheses to indicate uncertainty about the correctness of a number or date included in the sentence.
Exclamation Point (!)	An exclamation point is used at the end of a sentence, clause, phrase, or single word to express strong emotion.

Be aware that commas, semicolons, and question marks are not the only punctuation marks used within a sentence. However, because they are used more frequently than others, we will concentrate on them at this time.

Punctuation within a Sentence

Punctuation Mark	Usage
Comma (,)	Commas are the most common marks of punctuation within a sentence, and adding unnecessary commas or omitting necessary ones can confuse a reader and obscure the meaning of a sentence.

Semicolon (;)	A semicolon is used to separate parts of a sentence, such as independent clauses, items in a series, and explanations or summaries from the main clause.
Colon (:)	The colon tells the reader that the first statement is going to be explained by the second or signals that a question or series will follow.
Quotation Mark ("")	The main function of a quotation mark is to enclose a direct quotation. They are always used in pairs to mark the beginning and the end of a quotation.

Subject-Verb Agreement

The subject-verb agreement rule says if the subject is singular, the verb must be singular also. And if the subject is plural, the verb must be plural.

Subject	Verb
John	Is
Mary and Joseph	Are
We	Are
They	Are
He, she, it	Is

Tense (Past, Present, and Future)

Past Tense: Something happened before the present time. The past tense indicates a completed action or a simple action that is over and done with (history).

Present Tense: The present tense is used to show time in various ways: action happening now, action that happens as a regular occurrence, action that is historical, or action in the present (now).

Future Tense: The future tense is used to show something yet to come. The future tense is indicated by using *shall* or *will*. The action has not happened yet, but it will in the future.

The Dictionary

A dictionary is a book of written words from A to Z that defines the meanings of each word. Mom, Dad, you should use the dictionary and teach your children how to use it to look up the definition of words they don't know. If you don't have one, buy one or go to the library. They also have reference books and etiquette books that teach acceptable social and behavior skills in a variety of situations. Use them to help your children gain knowledge and wisdom in these matters. Make sure your children use the library when needed.

Basic Mathematics

Mathematics is a science of numbers. Sometime we say math instead of pronouncing the whole word. There are five branches in the science of mathematics:

1. arithmetic: math that deals with numbers

2. algebra: a branch of math that deals with numerical and literal numbers in an equation form to find unknown values

3. geometry: mathematics of the relations, properties, and measurements of solid surfaces

4. trigonometry: math dealing with triangular measurements

5. calculus: higher math dealing with rates of change

Moms and Dads, your children need a good understanding of each branch of mathematics at the elementary and high school level so they can solve complex problems at the college level and beyond. Algebraic expressions are used in all branches of mathematical science. It is important that your children learn the many rules of algebra and remember them. Remind them to stay alert and ask questions when they don't know an answer.

When studying math, do not use a calculator to solve problems. You need to exercise your brain so it can grow in wisdom and knowledge as your body grows in strength and maturity. After you have solved the problem with your brain, it is okay to use the calculator to check it for accuracy.

Numbers

Introduce your children to the fundamentals of arithmetic by showing them how to add: (2 + 2 = 4), how to subtract (2 − 2 = 0), how to divide (4 divided by 2), or 4/2 = 2, and how to multiply (2 x 2 = 4). Don't forget to teach them behavior skills, such as learning how to be sociable with one another. We have composed the times tables for you to study if you don't know them already.

Teach your children the arithmetic and algebra fundamentals. You should have your children to practice the times tables until they can recall the answer to any multiple without hesitation. You may think you don't need to learn how to add, subtract, divide, and multiply because you have a calculator, but you need to be able to perform these functions mentally without the calculator. You may not have it with you at all times, and your brain needs the exercise.

Times Tables

2 x 1 = 2	3 x 1 = 3	4 x 1 = 4	5 x 1 = 5
2 x 2 = 4	3 x 2 = 6	4 x 2 = 8	5 x 2 = 10
2 x 3 = 6	3 x 3 = 9	4 x 3 = 12	5 x 3 = 15
2 x 4 = 8	3 x 4 = 12	4 x 4 = 16	5 x 4 = 20
2 x 5 = 10	3 x 5 = 15	4 x 5 = 20	5 x 5 = 25
2 x 6 = 12	3 x 6 = 18	4 x 6 = 24	5 x 6 = 30
2 x 7 = 14	3 x 7 = 21	4 x 7 = 28	5 x 7 = 35
2 x 8 = 16	3 x 8 = 24	4 x 8 = 32	5 x 8 = 40
2 x 9 = 18	3 x 9 = 27	4 x 9 – 36	5 x 9 = 45
2 x 10 = 20	3 x 10 = 30	4 x 10 = 40	5 x 10 = 50
2 x 11 = 22	3 x 11 = 33	4 x 11 = 44	5 x 11 = 55
2 x 12 = 24	3 x 12 = 36	4 x 12 = 48	5 x 12 = 60

6 x 1 = 6	7 x 1 = 7	8 x 1 = 8	9 x 1 = 9
6 x 2 = 12	7 x 2 = 14	8 x 2 = 16	9 x 2 = 18
6 x 3 = 18	7 x 3 = 21	8 x 3 = 24	9 x 3 = 27
6 x 4 = 24	7 x 4 = 28	8 x 4 = 32	9 x 4 = 36
6 x 5 = 30	7 x 5 = 35	8 x 5 = 40	9 x 5 = 45
6 x 6 = 36	7 x 6 = 42	8 x 6 = 48	9 x 6 = 54
6 x 7 = 42	7 x 7 = 49	8 x 7 = 56	9 x 7 = 63
6 x 8 = 48	7 x 8 = 56	8 x 8 = 64	9 x 8 = 72
6 x 9 = 54	7 x 9 = 63	8 x 9 = 72	9 x 9 = 81
6 x 10 = 60	7 x 10 = 70	8 x 10 = 80	9 x 10 = 90
6 x 11 = 66	7 x 11 = 77	8 x 11 = 88	9 x 11 = 99
6 x 12 = 72	7 x 12 = 84	8 x 12 = 96	9 x 12 = 108

10 x 1 = 10	11 x 1 = 11	12 x 1 = 12
10 x 2 – 20	11 x 2 = 22	12 x 2 = 24
10 x 3 = 30	11 x 3 = 33	12 x 3 = 36
10 x 4 = 40	11 x 4 = 44	12 x 4 = 48
10 x 5 = 50	11 x 5 = 55	12 x 5 = 60
10 x 6 = 60	11 x 6 = 66	12 x 6 = 72
10 x 7 = 70	11 x 7 =77	12 x 7 = 84
10 x 8 = 80	11 x 8 = 88	12 x 8 = 96
10 x 9 = 90	11 x 9 = 99	12 x 9 = 108
10 x 10 = 100	11 x 10 = 110	12 x 10 = 120
10 x 11 = 110	11 x 11 = 121	12 x 11 = 132
10 x 12 = 120	11 x 12 = 132	12 x 12 = 144

Basic Concepts of Algebra

Since I did not have algebra in elementary school, I did not know how to use literal numbers and numerical numbers together to solve an algebra expression when I entered high school. I was too ashamed to ask what I should do first to solve an equation. I want you and your children to understand the basic concepts of algebra. The only stupid question is the one you fail to ask the instructor if you don't know about what is being discussed. Make sure your children understand that.

If you haven't studied algebra, it is a good time to know that algebra consists of numerical numbers (1, 2, 3, etc.) and literal numbers (a, b, c, etc.). An algebra problem is set up in an equilateral format (meaning that one side of the equation is equal to the other side of the equation). Sometimes there are several unknowns (indicated by a, b, c, x, y, z, etc.) in an algebra equation. We will solve an equation with one unknown such as: $6x - 5 = 19$ and show you how it is done. The equals sign (=) separates one side of the equation from the other. One rule says whatever you do to one side of the equation, you must also do to the other side of the equation to keep the original statement equal. In this equation $6x - 5 = 19$, x is the unknown. We must find the value of x.

What Shall We Do First?

T here are numerical numbers and literal numbers in the equation. Another rule says we must move all literal numbers to one side of the equation and all numerical numbers to the other side of the equation before we can solve it. And $6x - 5 = 19$ mean (6 times the value of x) minus 5 equals 19. To *remove –5 from* the left side of the equation, we must add 5 to it, because $-5 + 5 = 0$. And if we add 5 to the left side of the equation, we must add 5 to the right side of the equation to maintain the equality of the original equation. Thus: $6x - 5 + 5 = 19 + 5$ or $6x = 24$

Then we must divide both sides of the equation by 6 as illustrated on your right to determine the value of x	$6x = 24$ $6x/6 = 24/6$ $x = 4$

You can check the problem to make sure that the answer is correct by substituting 4 for x in the original equation.

Restated: 6x − 5 = 19
6(4) − 5 = 19
24 − 5 = 19
19 = 19

Algebraic Expressions

Algebraic Expressions	What They Say
2 x 4	Two times four
(3) (5)	Three times five
Ab	A times b
7y	Seven times y
3(6)	Three times six
3 · 6	Three times six
3/2	Three divided by two
2(6 + 4) − 8	Two times the quantity (6 + 4) − 8 or 2 (10) − 8
15 − 3² + 5	Fifteen minus the quantity of three squared +5

Operations of Mathematics

In mathematics, the four basic operations are adding, subtracting, multiplying, and dividing. When you first learn to add, subtract, multiply and divide, you use +, −, x, and ÷. The plus sign (+) and the minus (−) sign are still used, but the x is not used because it can easily be mistaken as a sign to multiply. It is only used as a literal expression of an unknown in algebra.

Algebra is a wonderful subject to study, and it requires total attention if you are to master it. It is a necessity to study if you are to excel in any important pursuit in life. It will sharpen your mind like no other subject I've ever taken, and self-discipline is a requirement to excel in this subject.

Addition

When you add, you can add only like terms. Terms like 7, 3, 0, and 1/4 are like terms. Terms that use the same variable to the same degree are *like terms*, 4a + 5a +1/3a are like terms. A number and a variable are unlike terms. Terms that use different variables are unlike terms. You can add any number: 4 + 5 = 9, 4 + 6 = 10, and 3 +2 +7 = 12. You can also add variables as long as they are the same variable. You can add xs to xs and ys to ys, but you cannot add xs and ys. To add like variables, just add the coefficient. The coefficient is the number in front of the variable. In the expression 9y, 9 is the coefficient, and y is the variable. In the expression 1/2y, 1/2 is the coefficient, and y is the variable. Note how like terms are added to simplify the following expressions: Y +2y + 3y = 6y. And 3y + 6y + 2y = 11y.

Subtraction

You can subtract one variable from another variable as long as they are the same variable. Just subtract the coefficient and keep the variable. 6b − 2b = 4b, and 4a − a = 3a (Remember the coefficient of a is 1) and 4b − 4b = 0.

Multiplication

An x is seldom used to indicate multiplication. It is too easy to confuse x the literal number with x the variable. To avoid this problem, mathematicians use other ways to indicate multiplication: A single dot (·) between numbers says to multiply. Writing two literal numbers or a literal number and a numerical number next to each other is another way of saying multiply. 8a = eight times a, ab = a times b. Writing a literal number or a numerical number before a parenthesis says "multiply," a(c) or 5(3) says multiply numbers inside of parenthesis such as (5)(10) says multiply.

Division

T he division sign (÷) is seldom used to indicate division. Instead a slash mark (/) or a horizontal fraction bar (-) is used. An a above the slash mark with 3 below it (a/3) means "a" divided by 3, and (a/7) means a divided by 7. You can divide like and unlike terms in algebra. You can divide any two numbers: 6 divided by 3 = 2, 8 divided by 2 = 4. You can divide any two of the same variables: c divided by c = c/c = 1 (only if the value of c is greater than zero). Another rule states that zero cannot be divided by itself. You can divide any two different variables: b divided by c = b/c. There are many rules in algebra that must be remembered and obeyed if you are to calculate the equation correctly. Pay close attention to your instructor, and ask questions if you do not know the question or understand it.

Order of Operations

M athematicians around the world have agreed on a certain sequence of operations in solving equations. The order of operations rule is used to solve mathematical problems. Without this rule, several different answers would be possible when computing mathematical expressions.

The rule tells us how to simplify any mathematical expression in four steps. Do everything in parentheses first. In the problem 9(8 – 2), subtract first, and then multiply the product by six 9(8 –2) = 9(6) = 54. Compute the value of any exponential expressions. In the problem 6 3^2, square the three first and then multiply by six: 6 (3 x 3) = 6 (9) = 54. In the problem (8·3) – (2·4) are expressed as (eight times three) minus (two times four). Multiply eight times three and then multiply two times four. Subtract last. Thus (8 x 3) – (2 x 4) = (24) – (8) = 16. Add and or subtract. Start on the left and go to the right. In the problem 8 – 3 + 7 – 3, start with eight, subtract three, add seven, and subtract three: 8 – 3 + 7 – 3 = 9 or 5 + 7 – 3 = 9. For example: In the expression: 5(6+ 5^2) – 7. The order of operation rules says we must follow this example: First do all operations inside the parentheses or brackets, including computing any exponents. Second, multiply or divide from left to right if required. Third, add or subtract from left to right if required. When you solve a mathematical sentence or expression, it is important to do things in the correct order. The order in which you solve a problem may affect the answer.

Look at the following problem. 4 + 2(8) meaning four plus the quantity two times eight or 4 + (16) = 20. This same problem could have another answer if the order of operations rule were not followed. You read the problem as four plus two times eight, but does it mean that? Example: 4 + 2(8), meaning 4 + 2 times 8 or 6(8) = 48. This is incorrect according to the order of operations rule.

Sequence of Operations

First, compute the value of what's inside of the parentheses or brackets, including computing the value of exponents. Second, multiply or divide from left to right. Third, add and subtract from left to right.

Solving Equations with Addition

x − 6 = 3 x + 6 = 6 x + 0 = 9	You can solve this problem by adding 6 to both sides of the equation as shown at your left. x − 6 + 6 = 0 on the left side of the equation, and 3 + 6 = 9 on the right side of the equation.
x − 6 = 3 x − 6 + 6 = 6+3 x - 0 = 9 x = 9	Expressed another way, x − 6 = 3 when you add +6 to -6 on the left side of the equation it = 0, and when you add +6 to 3 on the right side of the equation, it = 9.

Either way you solve the equation the answer will always be the same

Solving Equations with Multiplication or Division

There are two ways to solve this problem; however, the quickest way for you to solve it is sufficient. First look at the equation to decide what should be done first. In the equation 4/5y = 12, eliminate the 5 by multiplying both sides of the equation by 5. Then the equation says 4y = 60 after multiplying both sides by 54/5y = 12. To find the value of y, divide both sides of the equation by 4, and when we do, it says y = 15 as illustrated below.

4/5y = 12 5(4/5/y) = 5(12) 4y = 60 4y/4 = 60/4 y = 15	To solve the equation, multiply each side of the equation by 5 to remove the denominator 5, then divide each side of the equation by 4 to find the value of y.

Lowest Common Denominators

x/4 – x/6 = 3 24(x/4 – x/6) = 24(3) 6x – 4x = 72 2x = 72 x = 36	Multiply both sides of the equation by the product of the denominators 4 and 6, which is 24, then subtract 4x from 6x, which leaves 2x equals 72. Then divide both sides of the equation by 2 to solve the equation as illustrated.

Check the value of x by substituting 36 in the original equation to see if it is correct.

The original equation: x/4 – x/6 = 3

36/4 – 36/6 = 3

9 – 6 = 3

3 = 3

Therefore, it is correct.

c/3 = 18 3(c/3) = 3(18) c = 54	We must remove the denominator (3) from the left side of the equation by multiplying both sides of the equation by 3 to solve it as shown at your left.

Properties of Numbers

There are four properties of numbers: commutative and associative properties of addition, commutative and associative properties of multiplication, associative property of multiplication, and the distributive property of multiplication over addition.

What Do These Properties Say?

The commutative or associative property of addition states that no matter what order you add two or more numbers, the answer will always be the same: 3 + 5 + 10 + 6 = 6 + 5 + 10 + 3 = 24, because 24 =24, and a + b + c = b + a + c because a + b + c = a + b + c. No matter what order they are arranged, the answer will always be the same. Subtracting is not commutative. The order of subtracting does make a difference: 8 − 5 is not the same as 5 − 8, and 10 − 3 is not the same as 3 − 10.

The commutative or associative property of multiplication states that no matter what order you multiply two or more numbers, the answer will always be the same. Written in a math equation, the commutative or associative property of multiplication (a) (b) (c) = b (a) (c). Multiply any two or more numbers (a) (b) (c), and the answer will always be the same: 8(10) = (10) (8) because 80 = 80, 3(7) = 7(3) because 21 = 21, and 2(5) (3) = 5(2)

(3) because 30 = 30. The distributive properties of multiplication mean a(b + c) = ab + ac.

Decimals, Percentages, and Fractions

Y ou must know how to convert a decimal into a percent or fraction, so study the following examples to understand how.

Decimal	Percentage	Fraction
1.	100 %	1/1
.50	50 %	½
.25	25 %	¼
.125	12.5 %	⅛
.0625	6.25 %	1/16
.03125	3.125 %	1/32
.015626	1.5625 %	1/64
.0078125	.78125 %	1/128
.0039062	.39062 %	1/256
.0019531	.19531 %	1/512

The line items in each adjacent column expressed in decimals, percentages, or fractions are equal in value. To change a decimal or whole number into a percentage, move the decimal two places to the right and attach the percent sign (%) next to it as illustrated. To change fractions to a decimal, divide the numerator by its denominator. Let us use ⅛ as an example. The numerator is 1 and the denominator is 8. We know that 8 will not go into 1, so we must add 3 zeroes to the right of 1, and move the decimal three places to the right. Now we can divide. 1000. /8. 10/8 = 1, with a remainder of 2, bring down the second 0 to make it 20; 20 /8 = 2, with a remainder of 4, bring down the last 0, which makes it 40 40/8 =5 and point off three places to the left, therefore 1000/8 = .125 as a decimal, 12.5 % as a percent, or 1/8 as a fraction.

Proportion

If five pounds of potatoes cost $1.50, how much will thirteen pounds cost? To find out how much one pound costs, set up the equation thusly: Let n equal cost per pound. Then divide by 5 to find out how much one pound costs: $5n = \$1.50$: $5n/5 = \$1.50/5$. = $.30 One pound of potatoes costs $.30, thirteen pounds of potatoes cost (13) ($.30) or $3.90.

Answers To Questions You Should Remember

- What are literal numbers? Literal numbers are the alphabet, such as a, b, c, when used in an algebraic equation.

- What are natural or numerical numbers? Natural or numerical numbers are the counting numbers, such as 1, 2, and 3.

- What is a prime number? A prime number is a number whose only factors are itself and 1.

- What is a negative number? A negative number is a real number that is less than zero.

- What is the rule for subtracting sign numbers? Change the sign of the subtrahend and add, giving the sign to the larger number.

Math Shortcuts

This is a quick way of knowing the answer to any two-digit number ending in 5 without using the normal procedure to calculate the answer. For example, if a test question asked you to give the answer to 25^2. How would you do it? Usually you would multiply (25) (25) using the longhand method of multiplication to find the answer. Here is a quicker way to arrive at the answer. Add one to the first digit of the multiplicand, which is 3, and multiply it by the second digit of the multiplier (2) = 6, and attach 25 to the right of it as the correct answer, because the last two digits will always be 25. Let us square 65 using the example presented. If you said 4,225, you are correct: 6 x 7 = 42, and the last two digits will always be 25. Try any two-digit number ending in five and square it to see your answer. Let's say, 55, 65, 75, and 95. How did you do? (Check the answers at the end of this book.)

Fields of Study

There are many fields of study children can pursue: business management, psychology, medicine, biology, the humanities, chemistry, physics, engineering, mathematics, and many more. They should love whatever field they decide on! Don't worry about how much money is in it for them. Is it something they love to do? Can it help them achieve their goals?

People will go out of their way to subscribe to whatever you have to offer if it will help them achieve their goals. They will pay you for the privilege of subscribing to whatever you have to offer. This must be a sincere commitment to helping people achieve their goals.

"Verily I say unto you, Inasmuch as ye have done it unto one of the least of these my brother, ye have done it unto me" (Matthew 25:40). If we come together and produce the goods and services we consume, we can eliminate most of the crime committed in our communities. We can use some of the profits from these enterprises to improve conditions within it. This will give our young adults something to look forward to as an avenue to fulfilling their dreams.

An instructor at Lawson State asked, "Why should you go into business?"

Some said to make money, and some gave other reasons.

The instructor said, "You should go into business to provide goods and services to help people achieve their goals."

When the instructor said that, I recalled opening the gates for the truck drivers hauling logs. I created a demand for a service and fulfilled the needs of others in the process without knowing it. They paid me for it without me asking them! Give the customer goods and services they want at prices they can afford and let them know about it. They will beat a path to your door to get it.

Study biology—even if it is not required in your field of study. Take a few semester hours in it. Biology is the study of life, which gives insight into every living thing on earth—and how animals and plants work together for the common good of each other. It was a requirement that I had to take several semester hours of study in biology. I wondered what biology had to do with business administration. It was one of the most interesting subjects I had ever taken. If I had been a few years younger, I would have changed my major to biology.

You should expose your children to many art forms: painting, photography, public speaking, writing, and theater. When they are old enough, these experiences are worth their weight in gold to them. Children learn by observing action and reacting to what is going on in plays like "The Miracle Worker." They can visualize and understand that discipline and persistence can help them achieve their goals.

There are organizations that can help those who want a

second chance to get an education. Most public broadcasting stations offer free education programs. Check the website (PBS.com) to find out what subjects are being offered and the time they are being offered.

Another website, www.courser.com, at the time of writing this study guide offered anyone the opportunity to take the world's best college courses online for free. It offers 213 courses in categories that range from biology and life sciences to statistics, data analysis, and scientific computing. You can learn with videos, quizzes, assignments, and interactions with thousands of other students to advance your knowledge and career. You can contact Courser.com at 1-800-568-0045 or 607-739-3861.

The world is different than when I grew up, and it will be different tomorrow. You must see to it that your children learn to use the tools of the digital age and benefit from them because they are here to stay. There is some helpful information on television, but for the most part, there is not very much good information that is important to you and your children's future. Turn the TV off when you need to.

You can make it! I know because I've been there and succeeded! However, there is a requirement on your part: a persistent desire to get an education and the self-control to make it happen. This is the first step in achieving your goals. Without self-discipline, you will be facing an uphill battle in life.

You will be surprised by the financial opportunities an education gives you. It also provides opportunities to help others along the way. We want some things in life, and we need some things in life, but there are choices we must make. We need to know what things are most important in our lives and prioritize them in accordance with their importance. We must pursue them to their conclusions.

Discipline is doing the things you know must be done—and doing them when you know they must be done. As a grandson of a slave, the son of a sharecropper, and a child of God, I grew up in Mississippi during the Great Depression. Segregation was supreme, but I achieved my goals. Think of what you can achieve with the love of God abiding with you. There is no limit to what you can achieve if you think about what you want to achieve—and the reasons why.

The Schomburg Center for Research in Black Culture

515 Malcolm X Boulevard
New York, New York 10037-1801
(212) 491-2200
www.schomburgcenter.com

The Schomburg Center for Research in Black Culture is a research library of the New York Public Library. It offers many programs and exhibitions throughout the year that highlight black history for your education and enjoyment. You can contact the Schomburg Center at 515 Malcolm X Boulevard, New York, NY 10037-1801, (212) 491-2200, or www.schomburgcenter.com.

The Birmingham Civil Rights Institute

520 Sixteenth Street
North Birmingham, Alabama 35203
866-328-9696
www.BCRI.org

The Birmingham Civil Rights Institute provides a calendar of events and lots of helpful information. The galleries illustrate a brief history of descendants of African slaves struggling for freedom and justice in these United States. There are illustrations of segregated water fountains for blacks and whites, the Montgomery bus boycott, the struggle to vote, the door of the jail cell where Dr. Martin Luther King, Jr. wrote *Letter from the Birmingham Jail.*

Give Us the Vote is a film about the struggle to vote, and it depicts many more events, from the 1950s through the March on Washington in 1963. Its mission is to promote civil rights and human rights worldwide through education. The gift store sells CDs and books, including *Carry Me Home, Eye on the Prize, Until Justice Rolls Down,* and *Last Chance for Justice.* Memorable gift items include backpacks and miniature Congressional Gold Medals in bronze, which were presented posthumously to four little girls who were killed in the bombing of the Sixteenth Street Baptist Church.

Men, women, and children from all walks of life should visit the Birmingham Civil Rights Institute. Descendants of African slaves must know our history. Our history gives us the wisdom and knowledge of our past and a vision of what our future can be if we prepare ourselves for it as a coherent family that fights for rights and justice for all Americans.

The NAACP

P. O. Box 64983
Baltimore, Maryland 21215

4805 Mount Hope Drive
Baltimore, MD 21215
(410) 580-5777, (877) NAACP98
NAACP.org

The NAACP publishes the *Vanguard,* which keeps us informed about its efforts to fight against racial profiling and stop-and-frisk policies. We should support the NAACP and subscribe to this publication.

Our Federal Government

Our government is a democracy with a capitalist economic system; it is guided by a Constitution, mandated by the people and for the people. The Constitution is the system of laws and principles that prescribes the nature, functions, and limits of an institution.

> We the people of the United States, in Order to form a more perfect Union, establish Justice, insure domestic Tranquility, provide for the common defense, and secure the Blessing of Liberty to ourselves and our Posterity, do ordain and establish this Constitution for the United States of America.

Under the Constitution of the United States, the government has the authority to coin money, regulate commerce, raise taxes, and declare war. I encourage you to study the Constitution so you will know the government's duties and responsibilities.

Branches of Government

There are three branches of government: the executive branch, the legislative branch, and the judicial branch. Article II, Section two of the Constitution defines the president as the executive branch of government. Presidential powers and duties include: Commander-In-Chief of the Armed Forces, grant reprieves and pardons, appoint ambassadors and judges of the Supreme Court, take care that the laws of the United States are faithfully executed, advise and consent to congress on matters that are in the best interests of the people, and veto proposals presented by the legislative branch that are not in the best interests of the people.

Article I of the Constitution established the legislative branch. The legislative branch consists of the House of Representatives and the Senate, which form the United States Congress. The House of Representatives is made up of 435 elected members divided among the fifty states in proportion to their total populations. Members of the House are elected every two years. They must be at least twenty-five years old and be United States citizens. Congress has the exclusive power to introduce a revenue bill, impeach federal officials, and elect the president in case of a tie vote in the Electoral College.

The Senate is composed of one hundred senators (two for each state). The people of each state elect them every two years for six-year terms. Senators must be United States citizens and be at least thirty years old. The vice president serves as the president of the Senate and may cast the deciding vote in case of a tie. The Senate has the sole power to confirm presidential appointments that require consent and to ratify treaties. In order to send legislation to the president for a signature, the House and Senate must pass the same bill with a majority vote. If the president vetoes a bill, they may override the veto by passing the bill again in each chamber by two-thirds of each body voting in favor of it.

The Supreme Court is the judicial branch of government. The Supreme Court is the only power of the judicial branch that is explicitly called for by the Constitution. It is the highest court in the country. The Supreme Court deals only with Constitutional matters. The Constitution guarantees the rights of each citizen of the United States, and the Supreme Court is responsible for deciding how these rights apply to specific situations.

Each state has three branches of government, a governor (executive officer), a Senate and Congress (legislative body), and a court system (judiciary body). City governments have a mayor (executive officer) and council members (legislative body) with the power to govern its affairs.

Departments of the Federal Government

The Federal Government has many departments, including the Department of State, the Department of Defense, the Department of Labor, the Department of Health and Human Services, the Department of Education, and the Department of Commerce. Each department has a specific responsibility and mission. They sometimes have positions to fill—doctors, dentists, nurses, scientists, mathematicians, and engineers—and are willing to pay tuition for students who fill these positions after college.

The only requirement after graduation is an obligation to intern or serve the government in your field of study wherever the government needs your service for a specific period of time, usually between four and six years with pay. You must apply to the departments that need those skills to be filled and are offering the scholarships. The government will look at grades to determine which students will get the scholarships. Hunker down, be the best student in your class, and compete effectively to win these scholarships. This is one way to avoid a large financial debt after graduation.

Another way is to have your state representative recommend

you for acceptance to one of the military academies: the Naval Academy, West Point, and the Air Force Academy. You can also join the Reserve Officers Training Corp (ROTC) in college and serve as a commissioned officer after graduation. You are obligated to serve in the branch of the military for a specific period of time after graduation with pay. You may want to consider a career with the military, which is not an unworthy cause.

Take a course in government in high school or in college. You need to know how your government is organized, the different departments, and the duties and responsibilities of all levels of government. This is your government. You elect members from your communities to represent you. Make sure they are doing their jobs in the best interests of the people.

When they are not serving the best interests of the people, call and let them know that you are not satisfied with their performance. Let them know why. Familiarize yourself with your government at all levels. Know who to go to for help with problems that need to be addressed. If you want to run for office, you will know what office to run for—and what contributions you can bring to the position.

Government Roles

At all levels of government, the people are the government. We elect members from our communities to represent us by placing their names on a ballot and voting for them. And if they fail to consider our best interests in office, we have the responsibility to recall them or vote them out of office. Some of our ancestors died to ensure that we have the right to vote. Don't take this responsibility lightly. One vote can be the difference between winning and losing an election.

Our government represents all the voting households in this country; we can change any law if it does not conform to our needs—as long as it does not infringe upon the rights of others.

The Constitution can be amended to conform to the needs of its people. Study it, make sure it lives up to its creed, and participate to ensure that it does. Our government representatives perform many administrative functions at every level of government. I encourage you to get to know your local representatives. Ask them to visit your school to explain the role and functions of their departments. Ask your teacher to arrange a field trip to a local government function so you can understand what the government is all about and how it goes about the business of governing. There is a wealth of information at your local library on this subject. Ask your teacher to take your class to the library so you can access information on important subjects. Make sure you learn how to acquire information from your library, and use the Internet if the library offers it.

Our Economic System

O ur economy is set up as a capitalist system so individuals can establish privately owned or publicly owned companies and invest money in them. The state and the Securities and Exchange Commission regulate them with laws. Some elected officials have not enforced the laws to protect small investors. It has been said that some wealthier individuals have bribed elected officials to ignore certain laws and gain wealth at the expense of less fortunate investors. We must put an end to this kind of behavior.

An individual or group of individuals can go into business by petitioning the state to do business as a sole proprietor or as a corporation by applying for a license to do so. A sole proprietor is liable beyond the limits of its assets, but a corporation is liable only to the extent of its assets. The law says a corporation is like an artificial person. Fear not; the law provides each a means to file for bankruptcy protection.

There is no limit to who can go into business. In fact, the government encourages competition. During segregation, black people owned banks, hotels, restaurants, insurance companies, social gathering places, farms, and manufacturing enterprises. What happened after integration? Did we not realize that in order for us to profit from enterprises we own, we must support them by buying the things they offer? I encourage you to study your government and its laws—and benefit from what it permits us to do.

After the 2014 Election

The Republican Party won the majority in the house and senate during the 2014 election. By funding the federal government for the next fiscal year, it eliminated provisions of the Dodd-Frank Act, which protected small investors while authorizing a provision to allowed banks to take excessive risks by using credit default swaps. This provision brought our economy down to its lowest level since the Great Depression.

Large banks and corporations use lobbyists with deep pockets to influence elected officials. They make decisions that are favorable to them—at the expense of taxpayers if they fail

We cannot allow our elected representatives to favor corporations over those who elected them. This is another reason descendants of African slaves must come together: to produce and manufacture the things we consume. We need control over financial resources to eliminate these activities. The Constitution says that all people are subjected to the same rules of law—and that no one should be given preferential treatment over another.

Corporations owned by descendants of African slaves should not be a part of the Wall Street environment; this can be done by not listing their shares on any exchange. This would eliminate option trading or selling shares short in those corporations. There was a time when you could only sell a share short in a publicly traded corporation at least ⅛ of a point ($.12.5) higher than the last trade, which was known as the "Uptick Rule." The average investor who read the ticker tape could tell when short selling was taking place in any company because there would be an uptick or a downtick in every other trade. The elected officials eliminated that provision, which put small investors at a disadvantage. This provision must be reinstated if the small investor is to have a fair chance.

Contact Your Representatives when Necessary

There is a time when it may be necessary to write your representative—the president, a congressman, a community leader, or a member of the board of directors of a corporation. Let them know your concerns about anything that needs attending to within their area of responsibility.

The President

Ask the president to set the best example of leadership for this country—and encourage other elected officials to follow his example. The president should present programs to the legislative body that are in the best interests of the people. The president should veto legislation that is not in accordance with the Constitution and in the best interests of the country.

Legislators who propose bills that will not solve the country's problems should be voted out of office.

The Legislature

C ongress members and Senators, lose sight of your political party when a bill is introduced to make laws that is in the best interest of the people. I believe that is what you were elected to do. When you are not able to do this, resign—and let someone else do the job. Love of country over love of party is the reason "we the people" elected all of you. Get with it—and do what is good for the country—because without a country, there will be no need for a party.

Some people refer to the first black president by saying, "I hope he fails. Let's make him a one-term president." This is not the proper way for any elected representative to be thought of. And to send our men and women to war and signing secret pledges not to raise taxes for it or provide for their welfare when they come home. This is not an acceptable option for the American people!

We don't need politicians who are more concerned with their own interests than those who elected them. We don't need politicians who are looking out for their own financial interests. This is not what America is about.

Corporate Boards of Directors

A board of directors is the highest governing authority within the management structure of any publicly owned company. They select, evaluate, and approve compensation for CEOs and protect the shareholders' interests. They ensure that stockholders receive a decent return on their investments, including recommending stock splits, sharing repurchasing plans, and issuing financial statements. If they can't see do this, they should resign or be voted out of office.

Corporate CEOs

The board of directors selects a CEO to manage, communicate, lead, and make decisions that are in the best interests of stockholders. CEOs inform the board of directors when something beyond their authority is required.

Perform your duties in the best interests of those you represent in accordance with what is best for them and this country. Wall Street is not an entity unto itself; it has a responsibility to Main Street, the people of this United States, and every shareholder in accordance with the laws set forth in the Constitution.

When credit default swaps are presented as valuable commodities for sale, and you fail to speak out publicly against them, you are the problem. Is anybody out there listening to what's going on in corporate America and on Wall Street? Will greed undermine the integrity of our economic system? Eliot Spitzer; Elizabeth Warren where are you when we need you—more than ever—to expose the greed and corruption in corporate America? It will destroy our economic way of life if it is not stopped.

Community Leaders

Find ways to communicate with one another because the households throughout this country are the pillars of our government. If we fail to come together and communicate with one another about what is best for our communities and country, how can we implement such ideas? It will never happen. Our children's futures depend on it, and they are the future leaders of America.

Think about all the children in the community; it takes a village to raise our children. Help those who are least among us. Let them know that we are aware of their needs and are working to help them by bringing them into the household of faith in God through our Lord and Savior Jesus Christ. It creates a better society and a better community with less crime and corruption. It gives each of us a positive attitude.

We can make it happen. Stop pointing fingers. We can find solutions to problems that divide us by sitting down and planning how to do it. Bring back the concept of the block captain. Communicate with one another about how we can make our communities and country better. Get to know your neighbors. If there is corruption within our communities, get rid of it by exposing it to the proper authorities.

Clergy

There is a need to evangelize in every neighborhood across this country. God commanded us to love one another as He has loved us. America is in need of leadership in the arena of moral persuasion.

> God made the world and all the things therein, seeing that He is Lord of heaven and earth, dwelled not in temples made with hands. Neither is worshipped with men's hands as though he needed any thing, seeing that he gives to all, life and breath and all things. And hath made of one blood all nations of men for to dwell on all the face of the earth, and hath determined the times before appointed, and the bounds of their habitation. (Acts 17:24–25)

> Therefore as brethren of the call to preach and teach God's Word teach each of us that God is love. Jesus told his disciples: Have faith in God. For vrily I say to you, That whoever say to this mountain, Be removed and be casted into the sea, and shall not doubt in his heart, but shall believe that those things which he says shall come to pass (Mark 11:22–23)

> If you have faith when you pray; you will be given whatever you ask for. Enoch had faith, and did not die. He pleased God, and God took him up to heaven. That's why, his body was never found. But

without faith, no one can please God. We must believe that God is real, and that He rewards everyone who searches for Him. (Hebrews 11:6)

Blessed is the man that endureth temptation: for when he is tried, he shall receive the crown of life, which the Lord has promised to them that love him. (James 1:12)

Abraham had been promised that Isaac, his only son, would continue his family. But when Abraham was tested, he had faith and was willing to sacrifice Isaac. (Hebrews 11:17–18)

Because of their faith, the people walked through the Red Sea, on dry land. But when the Egyptians tried to do it, they were drowned. God's people had faith, and when they had walked around the city of Jericho for seven days its walls fell down. (Hebrews 11:29–30)

Because Noah had faith, he was warned about something that had not yet happened. He obeyed and built a boat that saved him and his family. In that way the people of the world were judged, and Noah was given the blessing that came to everyone who pleases God. (Hebrews 11:7)

What else can I say? There isn't enough time to tell you about Gideon, Samson, Jephthah, David, Samuel, and the prophets. Their faith helped them conquer kingdoms, and because they did right, God made promises to them. (Hebrews 11:32)

If you have faith when you pray for sick people, they will get well. The Lord will heal them, and if they have sinned, He will forgive them. (James 5:15)

Let your light so shine before men, that they may see your good works and glorify your Father which is in heaven. (Mathew 5:16)

Jesus said. Heaven and earth shall pass away; but my Word shall not pass away (Mark 13:31).

Be drum majors for justice and be an advocate for equality for all people in this country and around the world

Preserve Democracy for All Americans

O ur government is based on a constitutional democracy. A democracy is a form of government in which supreme power is vested in its people and is executed by those we elect to represent us. When common sense does not prevail through reasoning for the common good of all with problems such as gun control, let us amend the Constitution to limit the kind of arms a citizen may legally possess.

Our children must be free from fear, particularly in the classroom. Teachers carrying guns in schools are not a solution to the problem. He who lives by the gun shall die by the gun. The Constitution applies equally to all persons with social quality and respect for the individual within the community.

The Constitution must have boundaries. The majority cannot trample the rights of the minority; elected officials cannot trample the rights of those who elected them. Therefore, it is necessary that the descendants of African slaves take up the banner that calls American citizens to take responsibility for our government. Demand that elected representatives live up to the oaths of their offices—not as a party but as representatives of the people who elected them for the good of the country. When they cannot carry out their duties in accordance with that oath of office, resign. If not, we shall recall them and elect someone who can.

We must demand that the Constitution and the Pledge of Allegiance be taught in our public schools so children will know what democracy stands for. We must advocate that we are a peace-loving nation that wants to live in peace with other nations. It's okay to align ourselves with other nations who believe that a free democratic government is the best form of government. An attack on our allies is the same as an attack on the United States of America.

We should not police the world; let us walk diplomatically among nations. We should carry a big stick but vow never to use it except self-defense, in defense of our allies, or in defense of helpless people governed by ruthless dictators. We cannot go back in history and change what has been done, but we can amend previous actions that will permit us to move forward as a nation of immigrants under God. This should include the real Americans, the Native Americans.

Descendants of Slaves and Descendants of Slave Owners

Descendants of African slaves must take the initiative to reach out to descendants of slave owners in a sincere, conciliatory manner. This will create a learning environment for the descendants of slaves and descendants of slave owners in a brotherhood of love.

All American citizens must be educated to preserve democracy as it is written in the Constitution. Democracy in America is slowly slipping away. We've come too far to let this happen to us. The framers of the Constitution knew it should protect those who are least among us. We must be sure that all citizens are protected equally by it; if we cannot help the many who are poor, we cannot protect the few who are rich.

I'm not asking for a handout because the only thing a handout does is take the initiative away from those who receive it. Descendants of African slaves cannot do this without owning businesses and generating funds that can make this happen. President Franklin D. Roosevelt said, "There's nothing to fear but fear itself."

Let us reach out to the rest of the world with a beacon of hope in a diplomatic way that will show how a free democracy is the best form of government for humankind. Our doors are open to helping them establish a democratic form of government, including freedom of the press.

We must remain the leader in technical innovation and set an example for the rest of the world. We cannot do this by hating one another without a cause or ignoring the avenues we must take to educate all of our people. Let us build an economy that will benefit all of us.

Answers to questions pertaining to any two-digit numbers
ending in five squared are 3025, 4225, 5625, and 9025.

Notes

Notes

Notes

Notes

Notes

Notes

Notes

Notes

Notes

Printed in the United States
By Bookmasters